four letters

l. lewis

To the ones who are in search of their voice, may these words flow through you as they did me.

May it shake you to feel the things you have yet to let go of, the moments that need to be released in order to grow.

Feel it, and let it go.

All my love, always.

– Lexi

I had to feel, in order to heal..

Free yourself from all that holds you captive.

l. lewis

I saw your fire, and I let it burn me alive.

l. lewis

I sat in the stillness
long enough for the subconscious
to finally break its silence.

And I, I haven't stopped telling you
my stories since.

Someone needs to warn you about that beautiful boy who appears out of nowhere, after you had just sworn off getting tangled up in another. How his eyes will pierce a hole through your heart, and it leaves a space only for him, no matter where he disappears to with time. How his fingertips trace the pieces of you that no one had ever explored before.

How his lips fit perfectly into your own, and for a second, you forget that the world is screaming around you. How you know he will always try his damndest to not let you see how much he loves the way you look at him. How after him, you will never be able to taste french pressed coffee on Sunday mornings now, without your stomach sinking a little. You will question everything you knew after you see the depth inside of his eyes.

And you, you will write all the words you never had the confidence to say when you feel that empty space ache. The piece of you that he took with him when he left. Someone needs to warn you, that you will be someone new after your soul crosses his path.

And from that moment on, you will look for his eyes in everyone you meet. Trying to fill a void, that only he can see.

I didn't know how heavy it was,
until I let it go.

I didn't know that I could have been free.

I could have been free from me,
the entire time.

l. lewis

I did what I do best.
I swept the broken pieces under the rug.
And I cut more of myself while doing so.

So maybe that's the reason?

You came and you left and stayed
for only a season.

And yet, I saw your face when the
leaves turned their change.

I saw your face in the heat of the
August afternoons, the light casted
it's shadows across my room.

And I saw your face, when all the
seasons lost their zest.

I saw your face, and now,
I can't remember the rest.

I never smoked growing up.
I was around it while I was with
friends, breathed in their second
hand, but never inhaled willingly.
And then, I met heartbreak.
And then, I met you.

When you read my words,
I see you, searching for yourself.
Hoping I write about your warmth,

and I did, and I do.

But don't forget, that you made
me just as cold too.

How I wish you sunshine,
on days that are hard.

And oh, how I wish you strength,
when you feel as if you're falling
apart.

l. lewis

I sketched your eyes
into every piece of art
I created but with words
and called it poetry.

My pain often paints itself rather
too boldly, and though I try to hide
it's screams, my eyes tell the story,
that I pray you never see.

l. lewis

And I'll keep an open ending,
in case the stars decide,
to bring you home.

I'll entertain your small talk.
I'll say all the right things.
I'll pretend there aren't still
words, that you never said.
I'll play your game, until this
bottle runs empty. But darling,
please know, you're not fooling
anyone.

Especially me.

I'm scared.

I'm scared of waking up to it not
being you.

I'm scared of the lonely, even amongst
a crowded room. I'm scared of letting
someone in, always knowing how it
will end. I'm scared of the silence that
comes with your absence, for it is
always the loudest. But most of all, I'm
scared that no one will ever make me
feel, like you. And I'm terrified to think
that you don't feel it too.

- the way that I do

The truth is, darling girl,
Not everyone will see the
world as you do.

For some, choose to walk the
opposite way of the storm.

While you, dance freely in the rain.
Letting the thunder guide your wonder,
while the lightening ignites your way.
Knowing a rainbow, always comes
after the grey.

— storms aren't meant to stay.

l. lewis

When you tell them about me,
be sure to paint our story so clear.
Tell them I was the one who you let
fall, and now that I'm gone, you
remember it all.

How you search for my eyes in
everyone you meet, hoping and
praying they bring you to your knees.
But tell them instead, it will always
be me.

That I was the one, you couldn't
set free.

Maybe he didn't fall like he claimed,
maybe he just loved the fact,
that you could never bring him pain.

- you care too much

And if they ask you why you fancy
the ocean so dearly, tell them how,
when you wanted to drown it showed
you the sun kissing the horizon.
The warmth, flooded your skin.
It lifted the heavy from your lungs,
all the while you sought to inhale its
depth, it reminded you to breathe
instead.

l. lewis

As I write these words
a tear runs down my cheek.
Let this be my voice,
when I'm too scared to speak.

I recognize those scars, for I have them too.
As do I see, all that you carry.

l.lewis

And I will love you through your storm,
And I will hold you through your thunder.

l. lewis

I have trained myself to love in silence.
But my heart reaps the screams of
everything, of everyone I stayed silent for.

And oh, how it's changed me.

May her rooted soul
within her own
reality open your eyes to see
the power she holds
within your own reality.

l.lewis

Be still. Let yourself heal.

I never knew how beautiful
simplicity could be.
Lying beneath that window in your
room, as we gazed up at the moon.
The light reflecting off your eyes,
I had never seen such a view.
You were staring at it, and I,
was staring at you.

I left our love, where hope once grew.

You seek acceptance in everyone you meet,
yet the only soul you have yet to seek,
is your own.

l. lewis

Your inner peace is more important
than the one you're seeking closure from.

- let them go

And he said,

"You are all the poems; I have
  ever written."

He looked at me like he was looking
for an answer, but he didn't even ask a
question.

We both smiled, hesitantly.
Mostly because we didn't know what to say or do
after that.

The emotions were so tense, that you
could feel the heaviness sitting on your
chest. It made it hard to breathe.
Not in a bad way though, but just
trying to figure out where to go after
that moment.

I have learned that sometimes,
"being" is enough.
"Being" present.
"Being" there.
"Being" whatever the hell it is,
with someone who makes you feel
weightless.

And trying to look for more,
is what brings a storm that could have

been avoided, rather than just
appreciating their presence, and what
light they do bring to you.

But I, brought a storm..

l. lewis

She alone, is a poem of her own.

Be hesitant as to who you let
underneath your umbrella.
For some, will only use you
until it stops raining.

— empathy

It's within those shades of blue,
that I always look for you.

— eyes

May their voice fade into that
"nothing" they said you'd become.

Let them stay miserable in that
darkness that refuses to see the sun.

— demons

I hope you choose to love people,
even when it's hard to.

— exhale the rest

l. lewis

I didn't want or need you to fix me,
I was just in transition.
And you just happened to be the soul
that shined the brightest,
while I, was at my darkest.

l. lewis

Sure. She is beautiful.
But, is her heart?

l. lewis

Sometimes that song will come on
and I'll think of you.

I wish I didn't, but I always do.

I knew I was changing when I no longer clenched my teeth while looking at my naked body in that reflection. When I exhaled, and my shoulders released its grip on me.

I stopped looking at the pieces of me that I once disrespected and always criticized. The pieces of me, that only held the physical aspects of me. I lifted my gaze, to meet myself. To look into my own eyes, and not break that trance until I found who I was looking for.

The tears, they started to fall faster than I could keep up with, but I didn't look away. Truthfully, I don't even think I blinked.

I'll never forget that moment, because for so long, I was intimidated by her, my own self. Afraid of her, scared of being her, terrified of what might surface. So, I buried her, for years. I let her suffocate, until I finally said, "no more." I cried to her and I told her, "I'm so sorry." Because I listened to the world, instead of her.

Since that day, I swore that I would take care of her. To love her. To respect her. To communicate with her again. And stop letting the world in.

l. lewis

It took a while to let you go.
For months, I looked for you in places
subconsciously.

For weeks I had to tell myself to breathe
to inhale the newness of this
unfamiliar normal, to exhale the past,
and everything I was holding on to so tightly.
Grasping the last bit of you and I, my hands
grew sore from it, my heart far too beaten.

I'm still mending it, but it's getting easier.

— maybe

Your love
tastes of alcohol,
and now, I'm drowning
within it all.

— feeling everything, and nothing

I thought the universe was desperately
trying to break me.

Until I realized, it is balance.

I think some people were meant to
come into our lives, just to leave.

Those people are the ones you meet a
little earlier in your story.

You'll remember them,
though more will come and go as they
did. But it will always be the ones
from the beginning chapters that your
heart will refuse to forget, and let go.

You will think of them, and that little
piece in the pit of your stomach will
ache, no matter how many years have
passed.

You will feel it just as strong as you did
the day they left. Because you were still
new to all this. You loved with absolutely
all you had, fearlessly. All you knew to be
honest, true, raw, innocent, and even a bit naive.

They paved the way you loved, the way
you showed yourself to another,
when you were still just learning about
yourself too. And when they go, you'll feel the
absence of another's love.

It will change you, for as long as your
heart continues to beat, to love.
Sometimes it will be for the better,
and sometimes you'll have to learn
how to love all over again.

There are so many chapters to this
love thing. But the ones who are meant
to leave, will always go. And you, will con-
tinue to learn...

Every. Single. Time...

Reminding yourself that maybe
you needed them, in order to
grow.

The moon watched as your
hands tangled my hair, as your
lips dripped a silent scream
that craved, "more."

— before you left

And then, there was you.
So tightly wrapped around my heart,
not even I could untangle what had
been my own.

— overgrown

Self-doubt once looked me in the eyes
And whispered, "You are not enough."

In which I replied, "Where did you come from?"

Years of learning about a soul,
that I didn't know at all. *My* soul.
Listening to others, as their words
unwelcomely creeped in, without
hesitation, and without an invitation.

Years of self-evaluation and
the determination
As to why, "You are not enough."

It echoed inside of my head.
Remembering all the words you said.

Self-love, begins at home.
Your childhood, the words that they
tell you when you're alone.
And forgetting that you will carry them,
even when you're grown.

Rebuilding a broken soul,
from the ones who were supposed
to make you feel whole.

And the question was finally answered,
"Where did you come from?"

In which self-doubt replied, "Home."

I come from the words you learned to
speak when you were alone.
The ones you listened to instead of
listening, to your own.
Your home. Your heart.

You listened to the ones, who tore
you apart. You are more than you
give yourself credit for.

You are you, and that is enough,
forget about the other stuff.

Keep yourself away from the ones
who only bring rain.
They are no good for you.
They only bring you pain.

Let the sun in. Let the rest go free.
Tell yourself, "I finally, love me."

l. lewis

We attract what we mirror.

— reflection

l. lewis

She loved like an ocean
and she will drown you,
   with her depth.

My girl...
Be love.
Be gentle.
Be kind.
But, if you must,
remind them that, you too

Breathe fire

Leave them craving your soul,
as what they most desire.

l. lewis

And I promise you this,
if you run into that darkness
where all your fears hide,
there is where you'll find your light,
hidden inside.

— comfort zone

I will never ask myself again to be
the person who I know, isn't me.

l. lewis

For when he tears you apart
with his words,
may you always have the strength,
to stay anchored.

"Poetic"

Is what you called me.
Not knowing the depth
of my words.

Not knowing that
soon after, you were
written within every
chapter.

— twin flame

I turned my nights
into something new.
And I danced with the stars,
instead of you.

— La Luna

I pray that someday soon,
I see you dancing again to a much
brighter tune.

With those sunflowers in your hair,
igniting the world around you.

With that radiating flame that you carry
inside of your old soul.

A world that has left you feeling
broken, and a little less whole.

Sunshine girl, always remember your
magic. For you, take the broken and make
it new. Not just for you, but for the world
that surrounds you. And you, are what
most strive to be.

My darling, take your growth and let
it set you free.

— My Sweet Kate

l. lewis

If I ask you to tell me
what you love most,
you'll tell me of another's love,
or somewhere you call home.
But, how long would it take you to say,

"Myself"

If I ask you to tell me of happiness,
you'll tell me of someone else.
How they made you feel it
somewhere along the way.

Or, maybe even something materialistic,
instead of looking for it on your own.
Finding peace in being alone.

And when I ask you who you are,
I pray you say,

"Enough."

We wanted different things.
Yet, even so, we did agree
on one thing in which
we both wanted, and that was,
each other.

l. lewis

If you are longing for more,
let your journey start with
what you hold as truth
inside of your heart.

I wrote you a letter today,
My hands could hardly keep up
with what my heart needed to say.

It flooded everything, my eyes too.
I didn't even realize; how much
I've missed you.

Because I buried you and I for so long
Trying my absolute damnedest to stay
away, to stay strong.

But today, someone spoke your name
Though it wasn't you they were
speaking to, my heart instantly went
back to you.

And the walls that I had built to stay
away from you, came tumbling
down at the simplest thought of
everything I once knew.

But I'll be okay, someday soon.
Truthfully, I'm doing just fine today.
But sometimes, and only sometimes.
I find you in places where our souls
knew each other long before our faces.
I keep that close, those intertwined
hearts.

No matter what, no matter how long
this world keeps us apart.

l. lewis

And love only hurts
when you try to make it your own.
When it isn't meant for you,
when they, aren't meant for you.

— move on

l. lewis

I wrapped you in lies and called you safe.

— foolishness

l. lewis

There are so many who would love,
to love you.

Yet here you sit, stuck on the one
you thought you knew.

You.
You were my warmth,
when the season turned cold.

l.lewis

You slid the book from my fingers,
moved your hands up my neck,
ran your thumb across my bottom
lip while you cradled my face in your
hands.

And still, there isn't a moment yet
that replays in my head as much
as that one.

I hope your soul chooses differently.

I hope you run into that someone that
makes you feel alive, when every piece
of your heart was just screaming,
begging you to survive. I hope you
wake up to the sunlight warming your
skin from the naked window pain.
I hope you always choose to drawback
the blinds at midnight, so you can lie
amongst the stars underneath the
moonlight.

I hope you remember the sun,
and how it burns brighter in the
midafternoon days of early fall...
eyes closed, soaking it in,
remembering it all.

I hope you are forever in love
with the ocean. How it's still foreign,
with so little known.

So, when you're older and a little
more grown, you can look back at
those moments that made you feel, more.

Realizing that within those seconds,
when time felt as though it were
standing still...

your soul chose
differently.

Reminding you
just how deep your heart can
truly feel.

Your absence was so loud that
when it finally reached me,
the echo shattered the ceiling above me.
And when it came crashing down,
it was so destructive that I am still lying
here trying to put the pieces of myself
back together again.

l. lewis

I love you now,
I loved you then.
And you know
my darling soul...?

I'll undoubtedly love you,
until the end.

— always

Your lips pressed so hard against
mine, forcing a love we could no
longer find.

l. lewis

I chose not to write about you
for a little while.

To me, that was still giving you
too much of myself, even after
you were gone.

I didn't want to give you anymore
words, because my words are all I
have left. And I put so much of myself
into every word I choose to spill on to
this paper.

I didn't want you to know that
even after the mess we made,
I still miss that smile.
But here I sit, letting my heart spill out
again.

Praying that maybe it will find you
Hoping that maybe by then,
the ink that was so used to bleeding
only your name, has finally run out.

"But what if the circumstances
were different?"

I found my voice starting to shake,
growing a little louder, but also
weaker

You turned to me, with those
apologetic eyes,

"I have a million songs for situations
like that. But all of them end with us
hoping for more.

Wishing it were different, ending like
this, ending like we didn't want them
to."

And you shut the door behind you.

l. lewis

Consciousness is growth.

It is not your place
to put someone else's
broken pieces back together again.
But it is your place to show them
kindness, in a world where
they may have only seen darkness.

l. lewis

What if
all you have,
is you?

And what if,
that is enough?

I burned every breath of your
words onto this paper.
I wrote it down,
I tore it out,
I ripped it apart with my
teeth.
I screamed your lies out loud,
so that I, could breathe.
I let a part of you die that
day, and I finally had the
strength to put it down and
walk away.

— closure

When I'm alone,
I dive into the thought of you.
Pulling you in, to dance between
the sheets.

And it wasn't supposed to be this
way, yet I tangled myself up in you.
Legs wrapped, waists pressed,
running my finger across your lips.

Grabbing your hands,
pushing them down my hips.

Oh, and those eyes, the
depth within that gaze...
leave me missing the
way we spent
those Sunday's.

— play with me

I want to feel you,
and the way your
tongue makes me
come, undone.

Your hands danced freely,
your tongue followed the beat.
I wrapped my hands in your
hair while you whispered,
I, "tasted sweet."

l. lewis

The clouds remind me of your bed sheets.

There are moments where you will
wonder if being so tender hearted is
worth it.

Where you'll question your own
kindness, for weakness. But there
are moments where these thoughts
will manifest themselves into the
true reality of everyday life.

Very few will cross your path who
transparently see you.

They will see your true intentions,
in all its rawness.

They will strip you naked from the
inside, finding the pieces of you
that most do not see. I hope you
find those souls, there are so few.

But they are just as true, as you.

I told you to love me harder.
So, you wrapped my legs around
your waist, ran your hand down my
spine, and reminded me,
to breathe.

l. lewis

When you surround yourself with
those who choose to only bring rain,
don't expect to find sunshine,
where there is only pain.

If there's one thing I hope you
remember, let it be the moment you
interrupted my laugh with my face in
your hands.

While your eyes screamed more
emotions than any words ever could,
right before you pushed your lips
against mine.

So, if there's something you take
away from you and I,
God, I pray it's that moment.
Because that's when I knew,
that you loved me too.

— raining

You know, you never saw me at my best.
When the sun continued to shine
past 5pm, refusing to rest.
When my skin was a shade warmer,
my hair whiter, freckles darker, eyes
brighter.

You never watched me glide around
barefoot, smiling at those summer
nights.

You found me at my coldest season.
Eyes that were lost, a heart that was
aching, in search of a reason.

I pray that one day, you'll catch a
glimpse of that warmth inside my
eyes, and it will take you back to the
moments we shared talking until
sunrise.

But, by then, I'll be dancing all
on my own.

No longer afraid of being alone.

l. lewis

My stomach burns of alcohol.
I drink to convince myself
that you and I are worth it all.

— convincing ignorance

l. lewis

My spine cracked in two,
so I dropped the weight of
carrying you.

- one-sided love

l. lewis

Why are you still watering a seed
that refuses to let your sunlight in?

l. lewis

It's the quiet ones that you should
listen close to.
For they have had years of practice,
observing, while learning.

— silently

How exhausting it is to pretend
that no matter who loves my
way, I always choose you in
the end.

— tired

l.lewis

I shouldn't have to fill my blood with
liquid courage to love you.

Yet you were the piece of art,
that completely tore me apart.

— I take it back

Not everyone is going to love
you like you do them.

You need to learn when
to walk away.

You need to learn that
somethings, some people,
just aren't meant to stay.

— acceptance

Sometimes I look at her and
wonder how I could ever compare.
The way I chose to love myself back
then, was so unfair.

— self love

l. lewis

There are days I wish I could
take it all back.

I would have just let you be, and
a simple smile is all you would
have seen.

But instead, I undressed my soul.
Exposing the broken pieces that
made me a little less whole

And I let you in,
And let you see,

the most sacred pieces of me.

— my mistake

As of right now,
in this moment,
you are neither my happy,
nor sad, but rather something
in between.

"I held my breath for you."

The naivety in letting
myself drown, for those
who submerged me.

l. lewis

Heading back home,
I watch you disappear
in the rear view.

You turn, hands in your
pockets, you don't look back.

Why don't you watch me go like I
watch you leave?

Does this burn for you as bad as it
hurts for me?

I want you to feel something.

I want you to see yourself in
the brightest of light. Watching
your own fantasies spill
out, messy and untamed. And
within its overflow and eruption,
it stops you in your tracks. That
inspiration becomes a reality.
It paints itself along that once
empty canvas. From black and
white, to bleeding with color,
in all its spectrums.

I want you to feel something

So, I set myself free.

Enough for you to see, that
I painted myself, and all that
I was hesitant to be.

I shouldn't be spiteful.
Yet, I beg the stars to only
let you feel distaste in what
you so badly wanted to feel
as delightful.

When I let you in, you reached
down, wrapped your fingers
around, and pulled me up
from all that I was rooted to.

You showed me something new,
a love I wasn't used to.

And when you were finished with me,
you threw me aside.

But what you didn't know is when
I found new ground,
I planted myself much deeper.

And since that day,
I no longer beg others like you
to stay.

— I am my own

You don't have to make a sound,
for your voice to be loud.
Those who scream,
only want to be heard.
But those who speak,
want to be listened to.

l.lewis

It fell like rain,
gradually, and then all at once.
And before I even had time to catch
my breath, I was drowning.

— your fling but my falling

l. lewis

You cut me open,
exposed my wounds,
and poured salt into the tender.
You kissed the exposed pieces,
in which you created, and still
shamelessly asked,
why I tasted bitter.

Listen.
Just be.
Let others come to you,
let them breathe,
let them speak.
Be the sun they crave when in need.
Be the warmth, the safety from their storm.

— it will come back to you

I fed you promises
until you were full on hope.
You fed me from a bowl
that was empty.

There's this picture of you,
and for some reason, I can't make
myself erase it. It shows you, and by
you, I mean the parts of you that I
adore most.

And they are radiating
in this picture.

Sometimes, I'll skim past it.
Mostly because I know I don't have
the capacity to feel it all at once,
especially on days that I know I
couldn't handle the heaviness.
But sometimes, I'll find it when I'm
not looking, when I don't have a
choice but to look at it, at *you.*

And there you are.
I never knew how many emotions
one could feel at once, yet it always
happens when I see this picture of you.

Sometimes, I'll catch myself smiling,
and sometimes, I'll catch myself staring
blankly...

Staring at this memory that I haven't
labeled as anything other than,

"You."

I went looking for it today,
and today,
I didn't smile.
I just stared at you, sitting there,
frozen in time.
And I just simply remember.
It isn't much, yet there is everything I feel.

Even still.

l.lewis

We all are stumbling around
this Earth in search of something
to numb the thought that love could
save us all.

l. lewis

Let me love me, so I can love you.

l. lewis

I counted the seconds
between each moment of silence
before you finally had the courage
to shred our love to hell.

Maybe I enjoyed him too much
because he reminded me of all the
things I had forgotten about myself.
So essentially, I loved being around
him because I found love within
myself again.

– with or without him

l. lewis

I sit in the shower scrubbing my skin
in hopes that it will numb it enough,
to forget your touch.

You asked if I remembered,
and I told you,

"A little.'

But the truth is,
I remembered all of it.
Every single moment,
because it was what I held
on to when you disappeared.

I didn't want you to know how much I
cared, when you weren't even mine,
and you never really were.

Pathetic, is what I felt, when you went away
so easily. As I would lie awake so many
nights, fighting myself to not pick up
the phone at 2 am, to call you.
But, I knew there was nothing you
would've had to say, that would've
made me feel okay.

So, I did my damnedest to try and
erase you. I went out, I drank too much,
wrote too many love letters to no one.
Yet the second someone else asked for

my attention, I couldn't
help but look for you.

So, yes.
I remember, "a little."

A little more than I ever
wish I did. Sometimes, for days.

And do you know what, bud?

I think I'll remember "a little,"
forever. Because you took so
much of my heart
with you when you left,
and left me with so,
little.

l. lewis

My eyes reflect my inside.

– tired

My feet were bruised from running
to prove, that I was enough
for you.

l. lewis

And for everything I have ever lost,
I have gained wisdom within my
solitude.

l. lewis

You desperately wanted to hold
a story of me.

But my love,
I am more than just a poem.

I am a novel.

I am all the things your eyes
simply skim over but fail to read.
I am depth, I am the vibration,
I am the voice you long to hear
And you will only realize my truths,
after you've put out my fire for you.

l. lewis

The ocean bathed my anxious
in solace.

"Exhale"

You were sewn into every piece
of what I imagined belonging
would feel like.

Yet, you tore yourself from
me at the seams.

— unraveling

And like the bees,
you'll seek that sweet
taste of honey in
everyone else
that didn't plant
flowers, for you.

— like I do

And I know you must already know,
but I'm writing these words down
to help ease my own soul.
So, I need you to know,
I'm letting you go.

— wishing you well, always

l. lewis

Never settle yourself to be a river,
when you hold the depth of an ocean.

l. lewis

Who are you now that you've rid
yourself of the ones whose presence
filled your heart with silence?

And if you finally decide to start
believing in something,
I hope its love.
But most importantly,
I hope it's yourself.

I wasted an endless amount of time afraid
of being fragile.

Much like glass when it shatters, we forget
to look at the pieces with a different per-
spective which is also, what it creates.

We only see it's ragged edges that become
dangerous, we forget to look at what those
pieces do within it's fall.
It's cracked surface casts a spectrum of
color on whatever light hits it's considered

Brokenness.

"You remind me of art,"

And art, is such small word, for
all the colors I saw in you. For all
the inspiration that flooded my veins.
All the music that rolled off your tongue
when I let you in.

When you took my hand,
and reminded me to dance again.

You used your words to slaughter me
And as spit flew, like the words you used
I began to learn with time, to silence you.
The words you screamed, as your lips
purged with shame, became my silent
insecurities.

And again, with time, I learned that your
words, had nothing to do with me.

Only you.

I am a victim of falling for your touch.
The way your eyes would beg for all of
me beneath you. The way my name rolled
off your tongue, oh, how I begged you to
speak it just once more.

But now, I lie awake
listening to that distant humming
of the world around me as they sleep.
Drowning in yesterday's memories.

– say my name

l. lewis

I thrived on the pulsating thought that once
I let go, and stopped white knuckling you
and I, the space that you held inside of me
would find its way back to you.

How foolish of me to believe that you
ever gave me more than physical intimacy.

l. lewis

I am an ever changing sea.

Do not ask me to be the me
of yesterday.

l.lewis

I spent so much time on telling you to be
you, that I forgot to tell myself to be me.

l. lewis

"But what if I can't find my way back?"

Then I was never home for you.

"I'll be seeing you."

Maybe... Maybe when we are a
little older. When life brings us both
to the same chapter, like the one we
met on before. When we were both chaos,
and lost timing, and clinging to "maybe."

But today, I am your disruption with my
words. And you, you are the silence that
cracked me wide open.

"Out of sight, out of mind."

Oh, but will you find me when
you aren't searching.

Little dove, my words have lungs.

I have seen the harshest of souls
damn love and all that it is.

But that's how I know it's real.
Because had they not felt love
They wouldn't despise it for its
counterpoint.

"It's not the same,"

I smiled. Exhaled. And as always, pushed away the thought of him. But, there are moments when the pieces of him break through.

Fragments.

And like shards of glass, they make their presence known. And he bleeds into my memory again.

— all I see is red

l.lewis

You painted us into a sunset.
And though I prefer a sunrise,
I've never been in such awe of
it, of you and I.

The colors, they flooded the sky
above me. And when the sun set,
when we set, the stars still hummed
of what was left.

But tomorrow, the sun will rise.
And, as will I.

Find a way to communicate with a
tongue that all will understand.
A language that is fluent for all to
comprehend.

It's love, it's loss, it's life.
And it's beautiful, and sometimes
broken...

But it's the moments we share,
the words spoken.

And if we can agree on one simple
thing, something we all share as a
human being,

It's the moments in which we speak
with this tongue.

The moments,
We Love. We Feel.
We Lose. We Gain.
We Live. We Grow.
We Rise.
All of us together as one.
Underneath the same stars.
Underneath the same sun.

- 4 Letters

l.lewis

(to be continued...)

Dear friends,
Thank you for reading along.
Thank you for listening, relating,
and growing with me.
This book was originally meant for
just myself and my own healing,
but I realize the power of words and
what they can do for us.

"I'm sorry this chapter is a heavy,
but I swore I wouldn't sugarcoat
these truths anymore."

And I didn't.
-XO
Lexi

#llewispoetry

Made in the USA
Columbia, SC
06 December 2019

84491550R00090